Heating
and
Cooling

Cody Crane

Content Consultant

Elizabeth Case DeSantis, M.A. Elementary Education
Julia A. Stark Elementary School, Stamford, Connecticut

Reading Consultant

Jeanne M. Clidas, Ph.D.
Reading Specialist

Children's Press®
An Imprint of Scholastic Inc.

Library of Congress Cataloging-in-Publication Data
Names: Crane, Cody, author.
Title: Heating and cooling/by Cody Crane.
Other titles: Rookie read-about science.
Description: New York, NY: Children's Press,
an imprint of Scholastic Inc., 2019. | Series: Rookie
read-about science
Identifiers: LCCN 2018027642| ISBN 9780531134078 (library
binding) | ISBN 9780531138014 (pbk.)
Subjects: LCSH: Heat—Juvenile literature. | Temperature—Juvenile
literature. | Weather—Juvenile literature.
Classification: LCC QC256 .C73 2019 | DDC 536—dc23

Produced by Spooky Cheetah Press
Design: Kimberly Shake
Digital Imaging: Bianca Alexis
Creative Direction: Judith E. Christ for Scholastic Inc.
© 2019 by Scholastic Inc. All rights reserved.

Published in 2019 by Children's Press, an imprint of
Scholastic Inc.

Printed in Heshan, China   62

SCHOLASTIC, CHILDREN'S PRESS, ROOKIE READ-
ABOUT®, and associated logos are trademarks
and/or registered trademarks of Scholastic Inc.,
557 Broadway, New York, NY 10012.

1 2 3 4 5 6 7 8 9 10 R 28 27 26 25 24 23 22 21 20 19

Scholastic Inc., 557 Broadway, New York,
NY 10012

Photos ©: cover right ice cream: indigolotos/Shutterstock; cover
center ice cream: Captured by Nicole/Shutterstock; cover left ice
cream: Butsaya/Shutterstock; cover pig: Image Source/Getty Images;
back cover: FamVeld/iStockphoto; 2-3: Frans Lemmens/Getty Images;
5: Daniel Grill/Getty Images; 7: Design Pics/Ron Nickel/Getty
Images; 9 top left: Rawpixel/iStockphoto; 9 top right: Ariel Skelley/
Getty Images; 9 bottom right: Jasper Cole/Getty Images; 9 bottom
left: FamVeld/iStockphoto; 10: JGI/Jamie Grill/Getty Images; 13:
VYCHEGZHANINA/iStockphoto; 15: Jupiterimages/Getty Images;
17: Kjell Linder/Getty Images; 18: Martina_L/iStockphoto; 19:
dima_sidelnikov/iStockphoto; 21: OlegDoroshin/Shutterstock; 22:
vladsilver/Shutterstock; 25: hadynyah/Getty Images; 27 top left:
Kyodo News/Getty Images; 27 top right: STR/AFP/Getty Images;
27 bottom: The Asahi Shimbun/Getty Images; 28 top: Picsfive/
Shutterstock; 28 center: Lucie Lang/Shutterstock; 28 bottom: Natali
Zakharova/Shutterstock; 29 aluminum foil: pioneer111/iStockphoto;
29 chocolate: Anteromite/Shutterstock; 29 marshmallow: Texturis/
Shutterstock; 29 crayon: Lucie Lang/Shutterstock; 30 top: Kjell
Linder/Getty Images; 30 center: JGI/Jamie Grill/Getty Images; 30
bottom: Ariel Skelley/Getty Images; 31 top: VYCHEGZHANINA/
iStockphoto; 31 center: OlegDoroshin/Shutterstock; 31 bottom:
FamVeld/iStockphoto; 32: Louisianatreefarmer/iStockphoto.

Table of Contents

Chapter 1

What's the Weather?

The sun shines brightly in summer. The **weather** is hot. You might splash in some water to cool off.

What else can you do in summer to stay cool?

Winter weather is cold. Ice may hang from trees. The ground may be covered in snow. You have to bundle up to stay warm.

What else can you do in winter to stay warm?

How hot or cold it gets outside
changes during the year.
That brings different **seasons**.

What is the
weather like
today?

winter

spring

summer

fall

9

Chapter 2

Warming Up

Heat can move. It travels from hotter things to colder things. Heat moves from the air into this ice cream. That makes the ice cream **melt**.

Heating things can cause them
to change in other ways, too.
Heating water turns it into **steam**.

Is the
steam
coming from
this pot hot
or cold?

13

Food changes when we cook it. Cookies start out as soft dough. But heat from an oven bakes them into crunchy treats.

How does cooking change other types of food?

15

Chapter 3

Keeping Cool

Cooling something can change it, too. Water **freezes** to form ice when it is really cold.

How did these rocks end up covered in ice?

17

Cooling things is useful.
Your refrigerator keeps food cold.
That way it does not spoil,
like this moldy strawberry.

Would you want to eat this moldy strawberry?

What types of foods do you keep in a fridge?

19

A **thermometer** shows how cold or hot something is. The red liquid inside is called mercury. When the weather gets warm, mercury expands. It moves up the thin tube. The opposite happens when the weather turns cooler.

Is this thermometer measuring a cold or hot temperature?

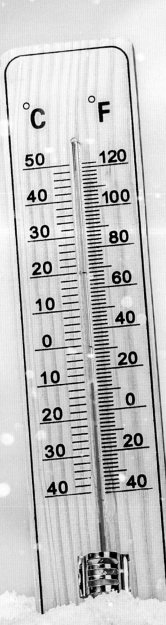

21

Chapter 4

Wild Weather

Some places on Earth stay
really cold all year long.
They are covered in snow and ice.

What animals besides penguins live in very cold places?

Other spots are *really* hot all the time. Deserts can be the hottest and driest places on Earth.

Do you think there is much water in a desert? Why or why not?

25

Some animals have fur to keep them warm. Others sweat or roll in mud to stay cool.
But sometimes nothing beats chilling out with a frozen treat.

How are these animals staying cool?

Will It Melt?

What objects melt in the sun's heat?

Remember to ask an adult for help with this activity.

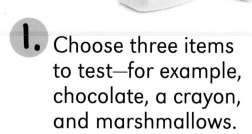

1. Choose three items to test—for example, chocolate, a crayon, and marshmallows.

2. Set each item on a piece of foil in direct sunlight.

3. Check on the objects every couple of minutes. Which melted fastest? Which took longest to melt?

What Happened?

Light from the sun gives off heat. The longer an object sits in sunlight, the hotter it gets. Different objects melt at different temperatures. For example, it doesn't take a lot of heat to melt chocolate. Crayons, however, melt at a higher temperature. They can sit in sunlight longer before melting.

freezes (**freez**-ez): changes from a liquid to a solid at a very low temperature

- *Water **freezes** into ice when it is really cold.*

melt (**melt**): change from a solid to a liquid at a high temperature

- *Ice cream will **melt** on a hot day.*

seasons (**see**-zuhns): the four natural parts of the year

- *Different **seasons** have different weather.*

steam (**steem**): the vapor (or gas) that water turns into when it boils

- **Steam** *rises from a pot of boiling water.*

thermometer (thur-**mah**-mi-tur): a tool that is used to measure temperature

- *Check a* **thermometer** *to see how cold it is outside.*

weather (**weh**-thur): the condition of the outside air at a particular time and place

- *The* **weather** *in summer is warm and sunny.*

31

Facts for Now

Visit this Scholastic website for more information on Heating and Cooling, and to download the Reader's Guide for this series:
http://www.factsfornow. scholastic.com
Enter the keywords **Heating and Cooling**

About the Author

Cody Crane is an award-winning children's science writer. She lives in Texas with her husband and son.